HALLE BERRY

Queen of the Screen-portrait of Determination and Hollywood Glory

Maxy M. Max

Halle Berry

Halle Berry

TABLE OF CONTENTS

INTRODUCTION

CHAPTER 1: WHO IS HALLE BERRY

Early life and upbringing

The Move to Hollywood

CHAPTER 2: BREAKING INTO THE INDUSTRY

The Breakthrough with "Boomerang"

Transitioning from Supporting Roles to Leading Lady

CHAPTER 3: ASCENDANCE TO STARDOM

The Role of Jinx in "Die Another Day"

Critical Acclaim and Awards Recognition

CHAPTER 4: CHALLENGES AND TRIUMPHS

Career Resurgence and Diverse Roles

Advocacy for Representation in Hollywood

CHAPTER 5: THE EVOLUTION OF AN ACTRESS

Personal Life and Advocacy

CONCLUSION

INTRODUCTION

Halle Berry's name resonates far beyond the dazzling lights of Hollywood. She is more than just an Academy Award-winning actress or a former beauty queen. Halle Berry embodies resilience, defiance, and an unwavering commitment to her craft. Born and raised in Cleveland, Ohio, she emerged from a childhood marked by challenges and discrimination to become one of the most iconic figures in the film industry. Her story is not just one of fame, but of battles fought and won—both personal and professional.

Berry's rise to prominence was not without hardships. The struggles she faced in her early years, from enduring racial prejudice to navigating the trials of a single-parent upbringing, forged in her a spirit that would one day conquer the screens of Hollywood. When many saw only her beauty, she showed them grit; where others might have faltered, she demonstrated unyielding determination.

Halle Berry

This book, Halle Berry: Queen of the Screen – A Portrait of Determination and Hollywood Glory, delves into the inspiring journey of a woman who shattered stereotypes and defied expectations at every turn. We explore the milestones of her life—from winning the title of Miss Ohio USA to becoming the first African-American woman to win the Academy Award for Best Actress in Monster's Ball. Through roles that pushed boundaries and choices that cemented her legacy, Berry redefined what it meant to be a leading actress in the industry.

CHAPTER 1: WHO IS HALLE BERRY

Halle Berry is an acclaimed American actress and former fashion model. She gained fame in the 1990s and has since become one of the most recognized and successful actresses in Hollywood. Berry is best known for her roles in a variety of films, including Monster's Ball (2001), for which she won the Academy Award for Best Actress, making her the first African-American woman to receive this honor.

Her other notable films include Die Another Day (2002), where she starred as Bond girl Jinx, Gothika (2003), X-Men series as Storm, and Catwoman (2004). Halle Berry's career is marked by her versatility, as she has played a wide range of characters in genres spanning drama, action, and thrillers. In addition to acting, she has also worked as a producer on various projects.

Berry's impact on the industry extends beyond her on-screen roles, as she has been a trailblazer for representation and diversity in film. Overcoming numerous personal and professional challenges, she has continued to maintain a respected presence in Hollywood.

Early life and upbringing

Halle Berry was born Maria Halle Berry on August 14, 1966, in Cleveland, Ohio, to Judith Ann Hawkins and Jerome Jesse Berry. Her mother, Judith, was a psychiatric nurse of English and German descent, while her father, Jerome, was an African-American hospital attendant who later worked as a bus driver. Berry's parents divorced when she was four years old, after which she was primarily raised by her mother in a predominantly white suburban neighborhood of Cleveland. This early environment would later shape Berry's resilience and understanding of race and identity.

Halle Berry

Growing up, Berry faced significant challenges. The neighborhood she was raised in was not always accepting, and as one of the few African-American children in her school, she often encountered discrimination and prejudice. Despite these challenges, Berry was determined to stand out positively and excel in whatever she set her mind to. This determination fueled her drive from a young age and pushed her to be a high achiever in both academics and extracurricular activities.

During her time at Bedford High School, Berry proved to be a standout student. She was an honor student, a cheerleader, the editor of the school newspaper, and even became prom queen. Her peers often noted her confidence, charisma, and ability to light up any room she entered. These attributes hinted at the path she would later pursue in show business, even though her early aspirations weren't initially tied to acting.

After high school, Berry attended Cuyahoga Community College, where she studied broadcast journalism.

However, she quickly realized that her true passion lay outside the confines of a newsroom. Encouraged by her natural beauty and poise, Berry decided to enter the world of beauty pageants. She found considerable success in these competitions, winning titles such as Miss Teen All-American in 1985 and Miss Ohio USA in 1986. Her participation in the 1986 Miss USA pageant further highlighted her determination and grace as she secured the position of first runner-up.

Berry's time in beauty pageants was more than just a step toward fame—it was an essential period that allowed her to develop self-confidence and public speaking skills, both of which would serve her well in her acting career. The pageants also introduced her to the glitz and challenges of the entertainment industry, sparking her interest in exploring it further.

However, Berry's transition from pageantry to acting was not without obstacles. After moving to New York City to pursue her dreams, she faced significant struggles, including periods of homelessness and financial difficulty. At one point, she even stayed in a homeless shelter when her savings ran out. It was during these tough times that Berry developed a deep resilience that would carry her through the ups and downs of her future career. Her mother's support and belief in her potential provided her with motivation to persevere despite the setbacks.

Halle Berry's big break came when she was cast in the television series Living Dolls (1989), a spin-off of the popular show Who's the Boss?. Although the show was short-lived, it provided Berry with much-needed exposure and led to further opportunities in Hollywood. Her first significant film role was in Spike Lee's Jungle Fever (1991), where she played a small but impactful role as a drug-addicted woman named Vivian. This role marked a turning point in her career, as it showcased her willingness to take on challenging, gritty roles that defied her beauty queen image.

Berry's early life was characterized by a combination of adversity, ambition, and resilience. Her experiences as a biracial child in a predominantly white neighborhood, coupled with the trials she faced as she broke into Hollywood, shaped her into a driven and dedicated performer. These formative years not only defined her work ethic and determination but also laid the foundation for her later achievements as an actress and advocate for diversity and representation in the film industry.

The Move to Hollywood

Halle Berry's journey to Hollywood was a combination of ambition, talent, and determination. Born in Cleveland, Ohio, in 1966, she spent her formative years navigating the complexities of a racially divided America. As a child of a white father and an African American mother, Berry often faced challenges related to her mixed-race identity. However, she was raised in a loving household that encouraged her aspirations, instilling in her the belief that she could achieve her dreams, no matter how daunting they appeared.

Halle Berry

As a teenager, Berry developed a keen interest in modeling and acting. After winning the title of Miss Teen All-American in 1985, she participated in various local pageants and eventually earned a spot in the Miss Ohio USA competition. Although she did not win, her participation caught the attention of talent scouts, leading her to pursue modeling opportunities in New York City. At the age of 17, she moved to the city, ready to seize her future.

While in New York, Berry faced the harsh realities of the modeling world, which included tough competition and a lack of consistent work. However, her perseverance paid off when she secured modeling gigs and began making a name for herself. She graced the covers of various magazines and appeared in advertisements, honing her skills and learning the ins and outs of the entertainment industry. Despite her success in modeling, Berry knew that her true passion lay in acting.

Halle Berry

In the early 1990s, after a few years of building her resume in New York, Berry made the bold decision to move to Hollywood. It was a pivotal moment that would shape the trajectory of her career. Leaving behind the familiarity of her East Coast life, she relocated to Los Angeles, where the entertainment industry was thriving and opportunities were more abundant.

Upon arriving in Hollywood, Berry faced significant obstacles. The transition was not as smooth as she had hoped; the competition was fierce, and she initially struggled to land substantial acting roles. Many casting directors viewed her primarily as a model rather than a serious actress. Berry took on small roles in television series, such as "Living Dolls" and "The Cosby Show," but these parts did not provide her with the recognition she sought.

Determined to break through, Berry immersed herself in her craft, taking acting classes and seeking mentorship from established professionals in the industry. She understood the importance of honing her skills to be taken seriously as an actress. Her hard work began to pay off when she landed a role in the 1992 film "Boomerang," directed by Reginald Hudlin. Starring alongside established actors like Eddie Murphy, Berry finally had the opportunity to showcase her talents on a larger platform.

"Boomerang" was a turning point for Berry. The film not only performed well at the box office but also introduced her to a wider audience. Critics and viewers alike took notice of her performance, leading to more opportunities in the coming years. Berry's transition from modeling to acting was solidified, and she proved that she was more than just a pretty face.

With her newfound success, Berry continued to push boundaries and challenge the industry's expectations. She pursued diverse roles that showcased her versatility, including dramatic performances in films like "Losing Isaiah" and "The Rich Man's Wife." Each project contributed to her growing reputation as a talented actress capable of taking on complex characters.

Halle Berry

Halle Berry's move to Hollywood was a testament to her resilience and unwavering determination. Despite the initial struggles and setbacks she faced, she never lost sight of her dreams. Through hard work, dedication, and a commitment to her craft, Berry transformed her career and eventually became one of the most celebrated actresses in Hollywood. Her journey serves as an inspiration to aspiring actors and actresses, illustrating that with perseverance and passion, it is possible to overcome obstacles and achieve greatness in the competitive world of entertainment.

CHAPTER 2: BREAKING INTO THE INDUSTRY

Halle Berry's rise in the entertainment industry exemplifies the blend of talent, hard work, and fortitude necessary to navigate the often-treacherous waters of Hollywood. While she initially found success in modeling, it was her passion for acting that propelled her to seek more significant roles and deeper artistic challenges. Her commitment to the craft meant that she was willing to take risks and invest in her growth as an actress.

In the early stages of her career, Berry was aware of the industry's expectations and the typecasting that often befell actresses of color. Many roles were relegated to stereotypes, offering limited opportunities for nuanced performances. Nevertheless, Berry approached each audition with a fierce determination to break through these barriers. She was resolute in her belief that she could redefine what was expected of actresses like herself, and she often spoke about the importance of seeing herself in varied and complex roles.

Her perseverance bore fruit with her participation in a series of diverse film projects. After "Boomerang," she starred in "Losing Isaiah" (1995), which showcased her ability to tackle emotionally charged material. In this film, she played a mother battling addiction while fighting for the custody of her child. The role required her to delve into the psychological and emotional complexities of her character, allowing Berry to display her range as an actress. Critics began to take notice of her talent, and she earned respect as a serious performer.

Berry's dedication to authenticity and her desire to portray characters with depth became defining traits of her career. She sought out roles that challenged her and avoided being pigeonholed into stereotypical portrayals. This determination was particularly evident in her later work, where she took on roles that depicted women facing significant adversity, often reflecting the realities faced by many women in society.

One of her significant milestones came with the 1999 HBO film "Introducing Dorothy Dandridge." This project was not only a tribute to the legendary singer and actress but also a deeply personal endeavor for Berry. She understood the struggles Dandridge faced as an African American woman trying to make her mark in a predominantly white industry. Berry's portrayal was layered and nuanced, earning her critical acclaim and establishing her as a leading actress in Hollywood. The role also marked her as a pioneer for other actresses of color, showcasing the power of determination and resilience in the face of systemic barriers.

Berry's performance in "Introducing Dorothy Dandridge" won her a Primetime Emmy Award nomination and a Screen Actors Guild Award, further cementing her status as a talented actress. The recognition she received opened the door to more significant opportunities, allowing her to transition seamlessly into mainstream Hollywood films. Her ability to capture the complexities of her characters resonated with audiences and critics alike, and she was increasingly seen as a force to be reckoned with in the industry.

The early 2000s marked a turning point in Berry's career, culminating in her performance in "Monster's Ball." The film, which dealt with heavy themes of grief, racism, and redemption, showcased her range as an actress. For her role as Leticia Musgrove, she underwent an intense transformation, both physically and emotionally. The depth of her performance was a culmination of years of hard work and preparation, and it was evident that she had poured her heart and soul into the character.

Her victory at the Academy Awards in 2002 was a watershed moment not only for her but for the industry as a whole. When she accepted the Oscar for Best Actress, she delivered an emotional speech, acknowledging the significance of her win for future generations of actresses of color. She expressed hope that her achievement would inspire others to pursue their dreams, reinforcing the idea that barriers could be broken.

Despite the accolades, Berry continued to face challenges within the industry. The road to stardom was not without its obstacles, and she often spoke candidly about the pressures of fame and the scrutiny that comes with it. Berry navigated the complexities of being a high-profile actress while also advocating for more substantial roles for women of color. She understood that her platform came with a responsibility to uplift others and was committed to using her voice to effect change.

Berry's journey into the film industry was not just about her personal success; it was about paving the way for others. She became an advocate for diversity and representation, pushing for stories that reflect the experiences of all individuals. Her influence extended beyond her performances; she actively sought to produce films that told meaningful stories and challenged the traditional narratives that dominated Hollywood.

Halle Berry

Breaking into the industry was a multifaceted journey for Halle Berry, filled with trials and triumphs. Her ability to navigate the challenges of being a Black woman in Hollywood and her dedication to her craft set her apart. With each role, she shattered stereotypes and opened doors for a more inclusive representation in film. Her story serves as a powerful reminder that passion, resilience, and a commitment to authenticity can lead to profound change in an industry that often resists it. As she continues to evolve as an artist and advocate, Halle Berry's legacy is one of inspiration, courage, and the relentless pursuit of excellence.

Halle Berry's rise in the entertainment industry exemplifies the blend of talent, hard work, and fortitude necessary to navigate the often-treacherous waters of Hollywood. While she initially found success in modeling, it was her passion for acting that propelled her to seek more significant roles and deeper artistic challenges. Her commitment to the craft meant that she was willing to take risks and invest in her growth as an actress.

In the early stages of her career, Berry was aware of the industry's expectations and the typecasting that often befell actresses of color. Many roles were relegated to stereotypes, offering limited opportunities for nuanced performances. Nevertheless, Berry approached each audition with a fierce determination to break through these barriers. She was resolute in her belief that she could redefine what was expected of actresses like herself, and she often spoke about the importance of seeing herself in varied and complex roles.

Her perseverance bore fruit with her participation in a series of diverse film projects. After "Boomerang," she starred in "Losing Isaiah" (1995), which showcased her ability to tackle emotionally charged material. In this film, she played a mother battling addiction while fighting for the custody of her child. The role required her to delve into the psychological and emotional complexities of her character, allowing Berry to display her range as an actress. Critics began to take notice of her talent, and she earned respect as a serious performer.

Berry's dedication to authenticity and her desire to portray characters with depth became defining traits of her career. She sought out roles that challenged her and avoided being pigeonholed into stereotypical portrayals. This determination was particularly evident in her later work, where she took on roles that depicted women facing significant adversity, often reflecting the realities faced by many women in society.

One of her significant milestones came with the 1999 HBO film "Introducing Dorothy Dandridge." This project was not only a tribute to the legendary singer and actress but also a deeply personal endeavor for Berry. She understood the struggles Dandridge faced as an African American woman trying to make her mark in a predominantly white industry. Berry's portrayal was layered and nuanced, earning her critical acclaim and establishing her as a leading actress in Hollywood. The role also marked her as a pioneer for other actresses of color, showcasing the power of determination and resilience in the face of systemic barriers.

Berry's performance in "Introducing Dorothy Dandridge" won her a Primetime Emmy Award nomination and a Screen Actors Guild Award, further cementing her status as a talented actress. The recognition she received opened the door to more significant opportunities, allowing her to transition seamlessly into mainstream Hollywood films. Her ability to capture the complexities of her characters resonated with audiences and critics alike, and she was increasingly seen as a force to be reckoned with in the industry.

The early 2000s marked a turning point in Berry's career, culminating in her performance in "Monster's Ball." The film, which dealt with heavy themes of grief, racism, and redemption, showcased her range as an actress. For her role as Leticia Musgrove, she underwent an intense transformation, both physically and emotionally. The depth of her performance was a culmination of years of hard work and preparation, and it was evident that she had poured her heart and soul into the character.

Her victory at the Academy Awards in 2002 was a watershed moment not only for her but for the industry as a whole. When she accepted the Oscar for Best Actress, she delivered an emotional speech, acknowledging the significance of her win for future generations of actresses of color. She expressed hope that her achievement would inspire others to pursue their dreams, reinforcing the idea that barriers could be broken.

Despite the accolades, Berry continued to face challenges within the industry. The road to stardom was not without its obstacles, and she often spoke candidly about the pressures of fame and the scrutiny that comes with it. Berry navigated the complexities of being a high-profile actress while also advocating for more substantial roles for women of color. She understood that her platform came with a responsibility to uplift others and was committed to using her voice to effect change.

Halle Berry

Berry's journey into the film industry was not just about her personal success; it was about paving the way for others. She became an advocate for diversity and representation, pushing for stories that reflect the experiences of all individuals. Her influence extended beyond her performances; she actively sought to produce films that told meaningful stories and challenged the traditional narratives that dominated Hollywood.

Breaking into the industry was a multifaceted journey for Halle Berry, filled with trials and triumphs. Her ability to navigate the challenges of being a Black woman in Hollywood and her dedication to her craft set her apart. With each role, she shattered stereotypes and opened doors for a more inclusive representation in film. Her story serves as a powerful reminder that passion, resilience, and a commitment to authenticity can lead to profound change in an industry that often resists it. As she continues to evolve as an artist and advocate, Halle Berry's legacy is one of inspiration, courage, and the relentless pursuit of excellence.

Halle Berry

The Breakthrough with "Boomerang

Halle Berry's breakthrough in Hollywood came with the 1992 film "Boomerang," a romantic comedy directed by Reginald Hudlin. This film was pivotal in shaping her career and establishing her as a leading actress in the industry. While Berry had appeared in various roles on television and in smaller films prior to "Boomerang," this project marked her transition into the mainstream, allowing her to showcase her talent alongside some of the biggest names in Hollywood.

"Boomerang" starred Eddie Murphy, who was at the height of his career and one of the most bankable stars in the industry. The film revolved around the character Marcus Graham, played by Murphy, a successful advertising executive known for his charm and womanizing ways. The story takes a turn when Marcus meets Angela, portrayed by Halle Berry, a confident and ambitious woman who challenges his notions of love and relationships. Berry's character serves as a foil to Marcus, and her performance was crucial in balancing the film's comedic and romantic elements.

When Berry auditioned for the role of Angela, she was determined to prove that she was more than just a pretty face; she wanted to be recognized for her acting abilities. The audition process was competitive, with many actresses vying for the role. However, Berry's charisma and ability to embody the complexities of Angela's character stood out. She brought a fresh energy to the role, blending humor with depth, which resonated with the filmmakers and ultimately secured her the part.

The release of "Boomerang" was a turning point for Berry. The film was commercially successful, grossing over $70 million at the box office, and it received positive reviews from critics. Berry's performance was particularly praised for its depth and authenticity. She portrayed Angela not just as a romantic interest but as a fully realized character with ambitions and desires of her own. This nuanced portrayal helped to challenge stereotypes about Black women in Hollywood, showcasing Berry as an actress capable of taking on significant roles in mainstream cinema.

The film's success propelled Berry into the spotlight and opened the doors to more significant opportunities in the industry. She transitioned from being a relative unknown to a recognized talent, gaining respect from her peers and industry insiders. Critics began to take notice, and her performance laid the groundwork for her future roles in both comedy and drama.

Following the success of "Boomerang," Berry leveraged her newfound visibility to pursue a diverse range of roles. She was determined to avoid being typecast and sought projects that showcased her versatility as an actress. The film not only boosted her career but also provided her with the confidence to take on more challenging and complex characters in the future.

Halle Berry

Berry's role in "Boomerang" was not only a personal triumph but also a significant cultural moment. The film contributed to a growing movement in Hollywood that sought to represent the experiences of African Americans more authentically and diversely. With its blend of comedy, romance, and social commentary, "Boomerang" resonated with audiences and was part of a wave of films in the 1990s that explored Black identity and culture in new ways.

In addition to its commercial success, "Boomerang" has left a lasting impact on pop culture. The film is remembered for its witty dialogue, memorable characters, and iconic scenes, particularly those featuring Berry and Murphy's chemistry. The movie has become a staple of the romantic comedy genre, and its legacy endures through its influence on subsequent films and the careers of its cast members.

Halle Berry's breakthrough with "Boomerang" also opened up conversations about representation in Hollywood. It highlighted the need for more diverse stories and characters, leading to increased demand for films featuring Black leads. Berry's success in the film served as an inspiration for other aspiring actors and actresses, showing that it was possible to break through the glass ceiling and achieve recognition in an industry that often marginalized talent based on race.

In the years following "Boomerang," Halle Berry would go on to further establish herself as a versatile actress, earning critical acclaim and numerous awards for her performances in films like "Monster's Ball," "X-Men," and "Die Another Day." However, it was "Boomerang" that laid the foundation for her illustrious career, marking her transition from television and smaller roles to the heights of Hollywood stardom.

Overall, "Boomerang" was more than just a successful film; it was a significant milestone in Halle Berry's journey as an actress. It represented her resilience and determination to succeed in an industry that often presents formidable challenges, particularly for women of color. The film's success helped to pave the way for

Halle Berry

Berry's future endeavors, solidifying her position as one of Hollywood's leading actresses and a powerful advocate for representation in the arts.

Transitioning from Supporting Roles to Leading Lady

Halle Berry's journey from supporting roles to becoming a leading lady in Hollywood is a testament to her incredible talent, resilience, and determination to redefine her place in the industry. After her breakout role in "Boomerang," Berry found herself at a crucial juncture in her career, poised to capitalize on the newfound recognition and momentum. However, the transition from supporting characters to leading roles presented its own set of challenges, especially for a Black actress in an industry that often struggled with diversity and representation.

Halle Berry

Following "Boomerang," Berry continued to build her career by taking on various roles that showcased her range and versatility as an actress. She appeared in films such as "The Rich Man's Wife" (1996) and "Losing Isaiah" (1995), where she played complex characters that required emotional depth and nuance. While these roles were significant in their own right, they were often overshadowed by the male leads, which highlighted the ongoing struggle for women, particularly women of color, to attain leading roles in Hollywood.

Recognizing the need to assert her presence as a leading lady, Berry was strategic about the projects she chose. She sought roles that not only challenged her as an actress but also allowed her to take center stage. This approach paid off when she starred in "Introducing Dorothy Dandridge" (1999), a biopic about the trailblazing African American actress and singer Dorothy Dandridge. In this film, Berry not only portrayed Dandridge but also produced the project, demonstrating her desire to control her narrative and the stories she wanted to tell.

Halle Berry

Her performance in "Introducing Dorothy Dandridge" was met with critical acclaim and earned her several award nominations, including an Emmy Award and a Screen Actors Guild Award. This role was pivotal in cementing her status as a leading lady and showcased her ability to carry a film, not just as a supporting actress but as a central figure. Berry's portrayal of Dandridge was not just a tribute to the late actress but also a reflection of her own journey in an industry that had historically limited opportunities for Black women.

The success of "Introducing Dorothy Dandridge" opened doors for Berry to take on more prominent roles, leading to her casting in "Monster's Ball" (2001). This film was a watershed moment in her career, as she played Leticia Musgrove, a grieving widow struggling with the loss of her husband. The role required Berry to delve deep into the complexities of grief, love, and redemption, allowing her to showcase her depth as an actress.

Halle Berry

Her performance in "Monster's Ball" was groundbreaking; it not only earned her an Academy Award for Best Actress but also made her the first African American woman to win the Oscar in that category. The recognition she received from the Academy and the film community at large was a significant turning point, establishing her as a true leading lady in Hollywood. Berry's win resonated beyond the awards circuit; it represented a victory for diversity and representation in an industry that had often overlooked the contributions of women of color.

As Berry continued her ascent, she took on a variety of roles that further demonstrated her versatility. She starred in major blockbusters like the "X-Men" series, where she played Storm, a powerful mutant with the ability to control the weather. This role not only solidified her status as a leading lady in action films but also showcased her ability to cross genres successfully. Her portrayal of Storm was groundbreaking, as it represented one of the first significant African American female superheroes on the big screen, further expanding the representation of Black women in mainstream cinema.

Throughout her career, Berry faced numerous challenges, including the struggle to find roles that were both empowering and meaningful. Despite her success, she often spoke candidly about the limitations imposed by Hollywood's narrow view of Black female characters. She remained committed to seeking out diverse and complex roles that reflected the multifaceted nature of Black womanhood. Berry understood that her platform came with a responsibility to challenge stereotypes and advocate for more substantial narratives that resonate with a broader audience.

Berry's transition to leading lady was also marked by her ability to balance commercial success with artistic integrity. She embraced opportunities to work with innovative directors and participate in projects that pushed the boundaries of storytelling. This dedication to her craft allowed her to evolve continually as an actress, enabling her to take on roles that reflected her growth and maturity both personally and professionally.

As she transitioned into a leading lady, Berry also sought to empower other women and marginalized voices in the industry. She used her influence to advocate for more diverse storytelling and representation, not only in front of the camera but behind the scenes as well. This commitment to advocacy was evident in her production choices and the projects she chose to support, as she sought to elevate the narratives of those who had historically been sidelined in Hollywood.

Halle Berry's journey from supporting roles to becoming a leading lady is a remarkable story of resilience, determination, and advocacy. Her ability to navigate the challenges of Hollywood while maintaining her integrity and commitment to diverse storytelling has made her a trailblazer in the industry. As she continues to take on new and challenging roles, Berry's legacy as a leading lady will undoubtedly inspire future generations of actresses to pursue their dreams and redefine their place

Halle Berry

in the entertainment landscape. Through her work, she has not only transformed her career but has also contributed to the ongoing dialogue about representation and inclusion in Hollywood, paving the way for a more diverse and equitable future in film.

CHAPTER 3: ASCENDANCE TO STARDOM

Halle Berry's ascendance to stardom is a captivating tale of talent, determination, and resilience in an industry that has often been challenging for women of color. Her journey from humble beginnings to becoming one of Hollywood's most recognized and celebrated actresses showcases not only her remarkable skills but also her ability to navigate the complex landscape of fame and success.

Berry was born on August 14, 1966, in Cleveland, Ohio. Raised by a single mother, she faced significant challenges during her childhood, including experiences with poverty and racism. However, her mother instilled in her the importance of education and self-worth. Berry excelled in school and developed a passion for performing arts, participating in various beauty pageants, which would later serve as a stepping stone into the world of modeling and acting.

Halle Berry

Her career began in earnest when she moved to New York City to pursue modeling and acting. Berry initially struggled to break into the competitive industry, taking on small roles in television and film. Despite facing numerous rejections and setbacks, she remained determined to succeed. Berry's first significant break came in 1991 when she landed a role in the critically acclaimed television series "Living Dolls," a spin-off of "Growing Pains." Though the show was short-lived, it provided Berry with valuable exposure and experience in front of the camera.

Her participation in pageants, notably winning the Miss Teen All-American title, contributed to her gaining recognition and respect in the entertainment world. This recognition was pivotal in securing her first major film role in Spike Lee's "Jungle Fever" (1991), where she played a supporting character. Although her role was minor, it garnered attention and praise from critics, establishing her as a promising talent. The film's success and its exploration of race relations in America provided

Halle Berry

Berry with an opportunity to showcase her depth as an actress.

Berry's perseverance paid off when she starred in the romantic comedy "Boomerang" (1992), opposite Eddie Murphy. This film marked a significant turning point in her career, as it not only showcased her comedic abilities but also demonstrated her capacity to hold her own alongside established stars. Her performance received acclaim, and she began to gain traction as a leading lady in Hollywood. "Boomerang" became a box office hit and solidified her position as a rising star.

As Berry's visibility grew, she strategically chose roles that would further establish her as a versatile actress. Following the success of "Boomerang," she took on significant roles in films such as "The Flintstones" (1994) and "Losing Isaiah" (1995), where she demonstrated her range by tackling both comedic and dramatic performances. In "Losing Isaiah," Berry portrayed a struggling mother trying to reclaim her son, showcasing her ability to convey deep emotion and complexity. This role garnered her critical praise and set the stage for her future success.

Berry's rise to stardom was not just about her performances; it was also influenced by her commitment to advocacy and representation in Hollywood. As a Black actress in a predominantly white industry, she faced unique challenges, including being typecast and struggling to find roles that resonated with her identity. Despite these obstacles, she consistently sought out projects that not only allowed her to shine as an actress but also highlighted the stories and experiences of marginalized communities. Berry recognized that her platform could be used to effect change, and she became a vocal advocate for diversity in film and representation for women of color.

In 2001, Berry's career reached new heights with her historic performance in "Monster's Ball." The film, which explored themes of grief, redemption, and love, provided her with the opportunity to showcase her dramatic abilities fully. Her portrayal of Leticia

Musgrove, a widow grappling with loss, earned her critical acclaim and the Academy Award for Best Actress, making her the first African American woman to win this prestigious honor. This groundbreaking achievement not only cemented her status as a leading lady but also served as a powerful statement about representation in Hollywood.

Following her Oscar win, Berry became a household name, taking on high-profile roles in major blockbuster films, including the "X-Men" series, where she played Storm, a powerful mutant with the ability to manipulate the weather. Her role in the franchise further solidified her status as a leading actress in action films, showcasing her ability to transition between genres seamlessly. She became one of the highest-paid actresses in Hollywood, proving that she could attract audiences and box office success.

Berry's ascendance to stardom is also marked by her determination to break barriers and challenge stereotypes. She became a role model for aspiring actresses, particularly women of color, inspiring them to pursue their dreams despite the obstacles they might face. Berry's story is one of resilience and strength, demonstrating that success is achievable through hard work, dedication, and a commitment to authenticity.

As she continued to take on diverse roles and challenge herself as an actress, Berry's influence extended beyond the screen. She became involved in various philanthropic endeavors, focusing on issues such as domestic violence, education, and health. Her work in activism further endeared her to fans and the industry, highlighting her commitment to making a difference in the world.

In addition to her film career, Berry has ventured into producing, seeking to create projects that resonate with her values and experiences. Her production company has focused on developing stories that highlight the voices and narratives of underrepresented communities, emphasizing her dedication to advocating for change within the industry.

Halle Berry

Today, Halle Berry is celebrated not only for her talent and performances but also for her impact on the film industry and her advocacy for diversity and representation. Her ascendance to stardom serves as an inspiring narrative for aspiring actors and actresses, showcasing the power of resilience, determination, and authenticity. As she continues to break new ground and challenge norms, Berry's legacy as a leading lady and a trailblazer in Hollywood remains firmly established, inspiring future generations to pursue their passions and strive for excellence in the arts.

The Role of Jinx in "Die Another Day"

Halle Berry's portrayal of Jinx in the James Bond film "Die Another Day" (2002) is a significant moment in both her career and the Bond franchise. Jinx is introduced as a strong, independent character who not only holds her own alongside the iconic James Bond but also subverts traditional gender roles often found in action films, particularly in the context of the Bond series.

"Die Another Day" was a pivotal film for the Bond franchise, as it marked the 20th installment in the series and was notable for incorporating modern themes, advanced technology, and a new direction for the beloved character of James Bond, played by Pierce Brosnan. The film is set against the backdrop of the South Korean and North Korean conflict, showcasing high-stakes espionage and thrilling action sequences. Within this context, Jinx serves as both a formidable ally and a compelling character in her own right, adding depth and complexity to the narrative.

Berry's introduction as Jinx is both glamorous and impactful. The character is initially presented as a Bond girl, but she quickly establishes herself as more than just a love interest. Her first appearance, emerging from the ocean in a scene reminiscent of Ursula Andress's iconic entrance in "Dr. No," immediately captures the audience's attention and sets the tone for her character. However, unlike many previous Bond girls, Jinx is portrayed as a capable secret agent with her own mission and agenda. This portrayal was a deliberate effort to modernize the Bond franchise and introduce a more empowered female character, reflecting changing societal attitudes toward women in film.

Jinx's character is marked by her resourcefulness, intelligence, and combat skills, which are showcased throughout the film. She is not merely a damsel in distress; instead, she actively participates in the action, holding her own against villains and engaging in thrilling combat sequences alongside Bond. This dynamic partnership redefines the traditional male-female roles seen in earlier Bond films. Jinx proves that she is as capable as Bond, challenging the stereotype of women as passive participants in the narrative.

Throughout the film, Berry's portrayal of Jinx emphasizes her strength and independence. Jinx is introduced as an agent of the NSA, tasked with uncovering the plot behind a dangerous North Korean general's plans. Her mission intertwines with Bond's investigation, leading to their eventual partnership. The chemistry between Berry and Brosnan adds an intriguing layer to the film, as they navigate their professional and personal dynamics while taking on formidable adversaries.

One of the most significant aspects of Jinx's character is her backstory and motivation. Unlike many Bond girls who often lack depth, Jinx is portrayed as a character with her own motivations and objectives. Her experiences as a government agent shape her character, contributing to her determination and skill set. Jinx's role goes beyond mere romantic interest; she is integral to the plot and contributes significantly to the film's resolution.

Jinx's character also represents a shift in the portrayal of women in action films. The early Bond films often relegated female characters to the sidelines or defined them solely by their relationships with male leads. However, Jinx's presence in "Die Another Day" signifies a broader evolution in the depiction of women in cinema, where female characters are allowed to be strong, independent, and multidimensional. Berry's portrayal of Jinx embodies this shift, as she navigates the complexities of her role while maintaining a sense of agency and empowerment.

Berry's performance as Jinx received positive reviews, further cementing her status as a leading actress in Hollywood. Critics praised her ability to blend charm and toughness, making Jinx a memorable character in the Bond franchise. Her role in "Die Another Day" not only showcased her talent but also demonstrated her ability to carry a major action film, proving that women can be both action heroes and complex characters.

Moreover, Jinx's character had a lasting impact on the Bond franchise and action films as a whole. Her portrayal paved the way for future female characters in the series, who were increasingly depicted as strong and capable agents in their own right. Jinx's legacy can be seen in the subsequent Bond films, where female characters began to take on more significant roles and contribute actively to the narrative.

"Die Another Day" was also notable for being the first Bond film to include a female character prominently featured in promotional materials and merchandising. Berry's presence as Jinx helped modernize the Bond franchise, appealing to a new generation of fans and showcasing the evolution of female representation in film. The marketing surrounding the film capitalized on Berry's star power and the character's strength, further cementing Jinx's role as a pivotal figure in the Bond universe.

Halle Berry's performance as Jinx in "Die Another Day" is a landmark moment in her career and in the portrayal of female characters in action films. By infusing Jinx with intelligence, strength, and agency, Berry not only challenged traditional gender roles but also redefined what it meant to be a Bond girl. Jinx's character embodies a new era of female representation in Hollywood, where women are no longer relegated to supporting roles but are instead empowered to take center stage as multifaceted characters in their own right. As a result, Berry's portrayal of Jinx not only left a lasting impression on the Bond franchise but also contributed to the broader narrative of female empowerment in action cinema.

Critical Acclaim and Awards Recognition

Halle Berry's career has been marked by an impressive array of critical acclaim and awards recognition, reflecting her extraordinary talent and versatility as an actress. From her early roles to her groundbreaking performances in major films, Berry has consistently garnered praise from critics and audiences alike, establishing herself as one of Hollywood's leading actresses.

Halle Berry

Berry's rise to prominence began in the 1990s, with standout performances in various television movies and feature films. Her role in "Introducing Dorothy Dandridge" (1999) earned her widespread recognition. Berry portrayed the legendary African American actress and singer Dorothy Dandridge, delivering a nuanced and compelling performance that showcased her acting prowess. This role not only garnered her a Primetime Emmy Award for Outstanding Lead Actress in a Miniseries or a Movie but also paved the way for her to take on more significant roles in feature films.

One of the defining moments of Berry's career came with her performance in "Monster's Ball" (2001), a powerful drama that explores themes of love, loss, and redemption. In this film, Berry played Leticia Musgrove, a widow who forms an unlikely bond with a prison guard, portrayed by Billy Bob Thornton. Her raw and emotionally charged performance was met with widespread acclaim, earning her numerous accolades, including the Academy Award for Best Actress. This historic win made Berry the first African American woman to receive this prestigious honor, a milestone that resonated deeply within the film industry and among audiences worldwide. The significance of this achievement extends beyond Berry herself; it symbolizes a broader movement toward greater recognition and representation of diversity in Hollywood.

Following her Oscar win, Berry continued to demonstrate her range and ability to tackle complex characters. In "Die Another Day" (2002), she portrayed Jinx, an empowered and capable character who challenged traditional gender norms in the James Bond franchise. Her performance received positive reviews, further solidifying her status as a leading lady in Hollywood. Critics praised her ability to blend charisma and strength, marking her as a standout in an iconic franchise. This role helped Berry transition from dramatic performances to action-packed roles, showcasing her versatility as an actress.

Berry's commitment to her craft and her ability to embody diverse characters continued to earn her accolades. In "Things We Lost in the Fire" (2007), she portrayed a widow navigating her grief while connecting with a man struggling with addiction. Critics lauded her performance as deeply moving and authentic, highlighting her ability to convey vulnerability and strength simultaneously. This role earned her nominations for various awards, reaffirming her position as a formidable talent in the industry.

In 2012, Berry delivered another critically acclaimed performance in "Cloud Atlas," a film that explores interconnected stories across different time periods. Her portrayal of multiple characters in various roles showcased her range and ability to inhabit diverse personas, earning her praise for her fearless approach to acting. Critics commended her willingness to take risks and push boundaries, further enhancing her reputation as an innovative actress.

Berry's work has not gone unnoticed by major award organizations. Over her career, she has received numerous nominations and awards, including Golden

Halle Berry

Globe Awards, Screen Actors Guild Awards, and NAACP Image Awards. Her success in both dramatic and action genres has made her a respected figure among her peers, and she is often cited as an inspiration for aspiring actresses.

In addition to her individual accolades, Berry's impact on the industry has been recognized through various honors celebrating her contributions to film and diversity in Hollywood. She has received the BET Award for Best Actress and has been inducted into the Hollywood Walk of Fame, further solidifying her legacy within the industry. These honors reflect not only her talent but also her role as a trailblazer for women of color in film, highlighting her commitment to advancing representation in the arts.

Berry's contributions extend beyond her on-screen performances; she has also been recognized for her philanthropic efforts and advocacy work. As a prominent voice for diversity and inclusion in Hollywood, she has used her platform to address important social issues, including racial equality and representation in the entertainment industry. This commitment to advocacy has earned her respect both within and outside the film community, as she continues to inspire future generations of actors and activists.

Throughout her career, Halle Berry has demonstrated an unwavering dedication to her craft, consistently delivering powerful performances that resonate with audiences and critics alike. Her ability to navigate diverse genres and complex characters has established her as a versatile and talented actress. The critical acclaim and awards recognition she has received are a testament to her remarkable journey in Hollywood, underscoring her status as a cultural icon and a source of inspiration for many.

In summary, Halle Berry's career is distinguished by her critical acclaim and numerous awards. From her early performances that set the stage for her success to her groundbreaking Oscar win and subsequent roles that showcase her versatility, Berry has solidified her place as

Halle Berry

one of the most celebrated actresses in Hollywood. Her achievements not only reflect her talent but also contribute to a broader conversation about representation and diversity in the film industry, making her a pivotal figure in the ongoing evolution of cinema.

CHAPTER 4: CHALLENGES AND TRIUMPHS

Halle Berry's journey in Hollywood is a powerful narrative of resilience, determination, and triumph over adversity. From her humble beginnings to becoming one of the most recognized actresses in the world, Berry has faced numerous challenges throughout her career, each of which has shaped her into the iconic figure she is today. Her story is not only one of personal achievement but also one that resonates with broader themes of struggle, perseverance, and the quest for identity in an often unforgiving industry.

Berry was born in Cleveland, Ohio, and grew up in a racially divided society that often marginalized people of color. Her early life was marked by hardship, including her parents' tumultuous relationship, which ultimately led to their divorce when she was just four years old. Berry's mother, a psychiatric nurse, struggled to provide for her and her older sister, often working multiple jobs to make ends meet. Despite these challenges, Berry's mother instilled in her the importance of education and self-reliance, values that would guide Berry throughout her life.

As a young woman, Berry faced significant obstacles in pursuing her dreams of becoming an actress. After winning several beauty pageants, including Miss Ohio USA, she moved to Los Angeles in the early 1980s to further her career. However, the transition was far from easy. Berry encountered the harsh realities of the entertainment industry, where she faced numerous rejections and was often typecast in stereotypical roles that did not reflect her talent or ambition. This period was marked by financial instability, and at times, she found herself homeless, sleeping in her car while auditioning for roles. Such experiences were profoundly challenging, testing her resolve and commitment to her dreams.

Halle Berry

Berry's perseverance began to pay off in the early 1990s when she landed a series of supporting roles in television and film. Despite this progress, she continued to confront the persistent issue of racial discrimination in Hollywood, where opportunities for African American actresses were limited. Berry often found herself competing against her white counterparts for the same roles, leading to feelings of frustration and isolation. However, she remained focused on her craft and was determined to break through the barriers that existed in the industry.

Her breakthrough performance came with the film "Monster's Ball" in 2001, which not only earned her critical acclaim but also became a defining moment in her career. Berry's portrayal of Leticia Musgrove, a grieving widow, was both powerful and transformative, showcasing her ability to convey deep emotional complexity. The film's success and Berry's subsequent Academy Award win for Best Actress marked a significant triumph, both personally and culturally. This victory was not just a validation of her talent; it represented a monumental step forward for representation in Hollywood, as she became the first African American woman to win this prestigious award in the leading category. The moment was celebrated as a breakthrough for diversity, inspiring countless artists and actors from underrepresented backgrounds.

Despite the accolades, Berry's career was not without its challenges. Following her Oscar win, she faced the daunting task of navigating the pressures and expectations that come with such recognition. The industry often imposes unrealistic standards on actresses, particularly women of color, leading to scrutiny over their choices and performances. Berry experienced this firsthand, as some critics were quick to judge her subsequent projects. The pressure to maintain her status as a leading actress led to several choices that were met with mixed reviews, and she often had to defend her artistic decisions in the face of public criticism.

Berry also faced personal challenges that impacted her career trajectory. Her relationships and personal life often became the subject of media scrutiny, which affected her mental health. The pressure of public perception can be overwhelming for any celebrity, but for Berry, it was compounded by her status as a Black woman in a predominantly white industry. She has spoken candidly about the emotional toll this took on her, emphasizing the importance of mental health and self-care in the face of such challenges. These experiences ultimately contributed to her advocacy for mental health awareness and her desire to use her platform to support others facing similar struggles.

Despite these challenges, Berry has continued to evolve as an artist and advocate. She has embraced roles that challenge societal norms and reflect her commitment to authentic representation. Her work in films such as "Cloud Atlas" and "John Wick: Chapter 3 – Parabellum" showcases her versatility and willingness to take risks in her career. Berry has also ventured into directing, making her directorial debut with the film "Bruised," in which she stars as a former MMA fighter. This project allowed her to explore themes of empowerment and resilience, both on and off the screen.

Throughout her career, Halle Berry has not only faced numerous challenges but has also triumphed over them, using her experiences to inspire others. Her journey is a testament to the power of perseverance, as she has continuously fought against the odds to achieve her dreams. Berry has become a beacon of hope for many aspiring actors and actresses, particularly those from marginalized backgrounds, showing that success is possible despite the barriers that may arise.

Her commitment to advocacy and her willingness to speak out on issues of race, gender, and representation have made her a significant figure in the ongoing conversation about diversity in Hollywood. Berry has used her platform to challenge stereotypes and promote inclusion, striving to create a more equitable industry for future generations of artists. She has become a role model not only for aspiring actors but for anyone facing adversity, demonstrating that resilience and determination can lead to extraordinary achievements.

In summary, Halle Berry's life and career are marked by a series of challenges and triumphs that reflect her unwavering spirit and dedication to her craft. From overcoming personal hardships to breaking barriers in Hollywood, Berry's journey is one of resilience, empowerment, and hope. Her accomplishments continue to inspire others, and her advocacy for diversity and inclusion in the arts remains a powerful testament to the importance of representation in shaping a more inclusive future.

Career Resurgence and Diverse Roles

Halle Berry's career resurgence in the 2010s and beyond is a compelling narrative of reinvention, resilience, and a commitment to diverse storytelling. After facing the challenges of navigating the industry's expectations post-Oscar win, Berry found new opportunities that allowed her to reclaim her status as a leading actress while simultaneously expanding her range through varied and complex roles.

The early years of the 2010s were pivotal for Berry as she sought to redefine her career following the intense scrutiny and pressure that accompanied her historic Oscar win. Many actresses find themselves pigeonholed after receiving such accolades, facing high expectations to consistently deliver award-winning performances. Berry experienced this phenomenon firsthand, and her initial post-Oscar projects received mixed critical receptions. However, rather than allowing this to deter her, she embraced the opportunity to explore different genres and narratives, demonstrating her versatility as an actress.

One of the key factors in Berry's career resurgence was her strategic selection of roles that challenged traditional stereotypes associated with female characters, particularly women of color. She took on a variety of characters that showcased her range, proving she could excel in both dramatic and action-oriented roles. In 2013, she starred in "The Call," a thriller in which she played a 911 operator who finds herself in a life-or-death situation when she must save a kidnapped girl. This role not only showcased her acting chops but also highlighted her ability to carry a film as a leading lady, proving that she could anchor a high-stakes thriller with depth and intensity.

Berry continued to diversify her roles with her performance in "Cloud Atlas" (2012), a complex narrative that intertwined multiple storylines across different time periods. In this ambitious film, Berry played several characters, demonstrating her remarkable versatility and willingness to tackle challenging material. Critics praised her for her ability to inhabit different personas and navigate the film's intricate narrative structure. This project marked a significant step in her journey, as it allowed her to work with visionary directors like the Wachowskis and explore themes of interconnectedness and the human experience.

Another critical success during this period was her role in "Frankie and Alice" (2010), in which she portrayed a woman with dissociative identity disorder struggling to find her place in the world. This performance was particularly notable for its emotional depth and complexity, showcasing Berry's ability to tackle difficult subject matter with sensitivity and authenticity. Her portrayal earned her accolades and nominations, including a NAACP Image Award, reinforcing her status as a serious actress capable of handling nuanced roles.

In addition to her film work, Berry also made a significant impact on television with her lead role in the series "Extant" (2014-2015). In this science fiction drama created by Steven Spielberg, Berry played Molly Woods, an astronaut who returns home from a year-long solo mission to discover she is pregnant despite having no physical contact with a man. The series explored themes of motherhood, artificial intelligence, and the human experience, allowing Berry to delve into complex emotional territory. "Extant" showcased her ability to lead a major network series while continuing to challenge the boundaries of her roles.

As her career continued to evolve, Berry sought to take control of her narrative by pursuing projects that resonated with her personally and creatively. This led to her directorial debut with "Bruised" (2020), a film in which she also starred as a disgraced MMA fighter trying to reconnect with her son. The film provided Berry with a platform to explore themes of redemption, resilience, and the struggles faced by women in male-dominated fields. "Bruised" was a labor of love for Berry, who worked tirelessly to bring her vision to life. The film received positive reviews for its raw and authentic portrayal of its characters, further establishing Berry as a multifaceted talent in Hollywood.

Berry's continued success is also evidenced by her foray into action films, where she has consistently demonstrated her physicality and dedication to the roles.

Halle Berry

In "John Wick: Chapter 3 – Parabellum" (2019), she portrayed Sofia, a fierce and capable assassin who assists John Wick (played by Keanu Reeves) in his battle against formidable foes. Berry underwent intense training to prepare for the role, showcasing her commitment to authenticity and physical performance. Critics praised her for bringing depth and complexity to the character, proving that female action heroes could be just as compelling as their male counterparts.

Her work in "John Wick" also highlighted a broader trend in Hollywood toward recognizing the importance of strong female leads in action films. Berry's portrayal resonated with audiences and showcased her ability to hold her own in a genre typically dominated by men. This resurgence in action roles marked a significant shift in her career, as she continued to challenge stereotypes while showcasing her versatility as an actress.

In recent years, Berry has maintained her momentum by taking on a variety of projects that continue to push her boundaries. Her role in "Moonfall" (2022), a science fiction disaster film, further cemented her status as a leading actress in diverse genres. In this film, she played a NASA executive who must join forces with unlikely allies to save the world from an impending catastrophe. Berry's ability to navigate different genres—from drama to action to science fiction—illustrates her versatility and adaptability in an ever-evolving industry.

Berry's commitment to showcasing diverse narratives and characters reflects a broader cultural shift in Hollywood toward greater representation and inclusion. Her advocacy for authentic storytelling has inspired many, encouraging a new generation of actors and filmmakers to push for more diverse representations on screen. Berry's own journey, characterized by resilience and reinvention, serves as a powerful reminder of the importance of perseverance in the face of adversity.

In conclusion, Halle Berry's career resurgence and her commitment to diverse roles have not only revitalized her own career but have also contributed significantly to the ongoing conversation about representation in

Hollywood. Through her choices, she has challenged stereotypes, expanded the possibilities for female characters, and demonstrated the power of resilience and determination. Berry's journey continues to inspire audiences and aspiring actors, reminding them that embracing diversity and authenticity is essential in shaping a more inclusive future for the entertainment industry.

Advocacy for Representation in Hollywood

Halle Berry's advocacy for representation in Hollywood is a central aspect of her career, deeply intertwined with her personal experiences as a Black woman in the entertainment industry. Her journey from an aspiring actress to an Oscar-winning icon has provided her with a unique perspective on the importance of diversity and representation on screen. Berry has consistently used her platform to champion the rights and visibility of marginalized communities, striving to reshape the narrative around who gets to tell stories in Hollywood.

Berry's advocacy began in earnest after her groundbreaking win at the 2002 Academy Awards, where she became the first African American woman to receive the Oscar for Best Actress. While the moment was celebrated as a significant milestone for representation, Berry recognized that it also highlighted the persistent issues of inequality and underrepresentation within the industry. In the years following her win, she has been vocal about the need for more diverse voices in filmmaking, emphasizing that representation is not just about visibility but also about authenticity in storytelling.

One of the key areas of Berry's advocacy is the portrayal of Black women in film and television. She has often pointed out the limited and often stereotypical roles available to actresses of color, advocating for more complex and nuanced characters that reflect the diverse experiences of Black women. Berry believes that

Halle Berry

authentic representation can challenge harmful stereotypes and provide audiences with a richer understanding of different cultures and identities. Through her own work, she has sought to break the mold, taking on roles that defy expectations and highlight the multifaceted nature of her identity.

Berry has also actively participated in conversations about racial equity in Hollywood, urging industry leaders to take responsibility for creating an inclusive environment. She has been a strong proponent of hiring practices that prioritize diversity, emphasizing the need for decision-makers—directors, producers, and studio executives—to reflect the communities they aim to represent. Berry has argued that the lack of diversity behind the camera ultimately affects the narratives presented on screen, leading to a homogenized view of the world that overlooks the rich tapestry of human experiences.

Her commitment to advocacy extends beyond her performances; Berry has utilized her visibility to support initiatives that promote diversity in filmmaking. She has partnered with organizations dedicated to empowering underrepresented voices in the industry, encouraging aspiring filmmakers and actors from diverse backgrounds to pursue their dreams. Through mentorship programs and public speaking engagements, she has shared her experiences and insights, motivating others to break through the barriers that often hinder their progress in Hollywood.

In addition to her work in front of the camera, Berry has embraced opportunities to shape narratives as a producer and director. Her directorial debut, "Bruised," is a prime example of her commitment to telling authentic stories that resonate with a broader audience. The film not only showcases a powerful narrative about resilience and redemption but also features a predominantly female cast and crew, highlighting Berry's dedication to elevating women's voices in the industry. By taking on the role of director, Berry has challenged the notion that women, particularly women of color, cannot lead projects at a high level.

Halle Berry

Berry's advocacy has also focused on the broader implications of representation in Hollywood, particularly in terms of its impact on society. She believes that film and television play a crucial role in shaping perceptions and attitudes toward different cultures and identities. When audiences see diverse stories and characters on screen, it fosters empathy and understanding, helping to break down prejudices and stereotypes. Berry has articulated the belief that diverse representation is essential not only for the entertainment industry but for society as a whole, as it promotes inclusivity and respect for all individuals.

Throughout her career, Halle Berry has navigated the complexities of being a trailblazer in an industry that often grapples with issues of race, gender, and representation. Her willingness to speak out about these challenges, coupled with her commitment to championing diversity, has made her a powerful advocate for change. Berry's efforts have contributed to a growing awareness within Hollywood of the need for more inclusive practices, and she continues to inspire a new generation of artists to push for authenticity in storytelling.

As the entertainment landscape evolves, Berry remains a vital voice in the ongoing conversation about representation in Hollywood. Her advocacy reflects a broader cultural movement toward inclusivity, where diverse stories are not just welcomed but celebrated. Berry's legacy is one of empowerment and inspiration, encouraging individuals from all backgrounds to pursue their passions and share their unique narratives.

In summary, Halle Berry's advocacy for representation in Hollywood is a testament to her dedication to inclusivity and authenticity in storytelling. Through her career choices, public speaking, and involvement in initiatives aimed at elevating underrepresented voices, Berry has played a crucial role in challenging stereotypes and promoting a more equitable industry. Her ongoing commitment to advocating for diversity serves as a powerful reminder of the impact that representation can have on shaping perceptions and fostering understanding in a diverse society.

CHAPTER 5: THE EVOLUTION OF AN ACTRESS

Halle Berry's evolution as an actress is a remarkable journey marked by transformation, resilience, and a relentless pursuit of excellence. From her early days in the entertainment industry to her status as a Hollywood icon, Berry has navigated a landscape that has not only challenged her talents but also shaped her identity as a performer. Her career trajectory reflects the broader changes within the film industry, particularly regarding the roles available to women, especially women of color.

Berry's entry into the entertainment world began in the early 1990s when she appeared in various television shows and films, initially gaining recognition for her beauty and charm. Her early roles often relegated her to the status of the love interest or supporting character, which is a common experience for many actresses, especially those from underrepresented backgrounds.

Halle Berry

Despite the limitations of these early roles, Berry's determination to break free from stereotypical portrayals fueled her desire to seek out more substantial and complex characters.

The mid-1990s marked a turning point in Berry's career. Her breakthrough role in "The Rich Man's Wife" (1996) showcased her ability to handle intense dramatic material, but it was her performance in "Losing Isaiah" (1995) that truly highlighted her acting chops. In this film, Berry portrayed a drug addict who fights for custody of her son, a role that demanded emotional depth and vulnerability. This performance garnered critical acclaim and set the stage for more challenging roles, signaling her evolution from a promising actress to a serious contender in Hollywood.

Berry's ascent continued as she took on more diverse roles, and she demonstrated her commitment to tackling complex narratives that resonated with her own experiences as a Black woman. Her performance in "Monster's Ball" (2001) was a defining moment in her career. The film, which dealt with themes of love, loss, and redemption, allowed Berry to showcase her extraordinary range as an actress. Her portrayal of Leticia Musgrove, a struggling single mother who finds solace in an unlikely relationship, was met with widespread acclaim, culminating in her historic Oscar win. This moment not only solidified her status as a leading actress but also marked a significant milestone in Hollywood, breaking barriers for actresses of color.

Following her Oscar win, Berry faced the daunting challenge of navigating an industry that often expects performers to continuously deliver award-winning performances. Many actresses find themselves typecast or burdened by the weight of their previous successes. However, Berry responded by consciously seeking out roles that would allow her to expand her repertoire. She continued to explore a variety of genres, from action films like "Die Another Day" (2002) to romantic comedies such as "Boomerang" (1992). Berry's willingness to embrace diverse roles reflected her desire to challenge the industry's expectations while demonstrating her versatility as an actress.

Berry's evolution also extended to her involvement in the production side of the industry. She began to take control of her narratives by producing films that aligned with her vision and values. Her work as a producer allowed her to advocate for more authentic representation of women and people of color in storytelling. This shift not only showcased her commitment to fostering diverse narratives but also marked a significant step in her evolution as an actress—transforming from a performer who interprets roles to a creator who shapes stories.

The evolution of Halle Berry as an actress is also intertwined with her experiences as a woman navigating the complexities of Hollywood. Throughout her career, she has confronted the challenges of ageism and sexism that many actresses face as they grow older. Rather than retreating from the spotlight, Berry has embraced these challenges and used them as motivation to pursue roles that reflect her maturity and depth as a performer. This determination has enabled her to continue evolving, adapting to changing industry dynamics while remaining relevant in an ever-competitive landscape.

In recent years, Berry's evolution has taken on new dimensions as she explores opportunities behind the camera. Her directorial debut, "Bruised" (2020), not only marked a significant milestone in her career but also allowed her to take charge of the narrative in a way she had never done before. In this film, Berry played an MMA fighter seeking redemption, reflecting her personal journey of resilience and determination. By stepping into the role of director, she demonstrated her multifaceted talent and commitment to telling stories that resonate with her own experiences.

Throughout her career, Halle Berry has consistently challenged herself and the industry to evolve. She has embraced the complexities of her identity, using her platform to advocate for greater representation and diversity in Hollywood. As she navigates new challenges and opportunities, Berry's journey serves as an inspiration for aspiring actresses and filmmakers, encouraging them to break free from the confines of traditional roles and explore the depths of their creativity.

In summary, the evolution of Halle Berry as an actress is a testament to her resilience, versatility, and commitment to authenticity in storytelling. Her journey from a young performer to a Hollywood icon reflects broader changes in the industry and highlights the importance of diverse representation. Through her work, Berry continues to inspire others to embrace their identities, challenge stereotypes, and advocate for more inclusive narratives in film and television. Her legacy is not only one of individual achievement but also a powerful reminder of the transformative potential of art and storytelling in shaping cultural perceptions and fostering understanding.

Personal Life and Advocacy

Halle Berry

Halle Berry's personal life has often been as captivating as her on-screen performances, marked by both triumphs and challenges. Her experiences outside of her professional career have shaped her identity and influenced her advocacy work, allowing her to connect deeply with various social issues. Berry's journey is one of resilience, navigating the complexities of fame while remaining committed to her beliefs and values.

Born on August 14, 1966, in Cleveland, Ohio, Halle Berry grew up in a mixed-race family, with her mother being white and her father Black. This biracial background has played a significant role in shaping her perspective on identity and race in America. Berry often reflects on the struggles she faced during her childhood, particularly regarding her racial identity. Growing up in a predominantly white neighborhood, she encountered prejudice and discrimination, which made her acutely aware of the complexities of being a person of color in a society that often struggles with issues of race. These early experiences laid the groundwork for her future advocacy for diversity and representation in Hollywood.

Halle Berry

Berry's personal life has also been marked by her relationships and motherhood. She has been married three times and has two children. Her experiences as a mother have significantly influenced her views on gender equality and representation in the entertainment industry. Berry often speaks about the importance of setting a positive example for her children, especially her daughter, Nahla, whom she shares with ex-boyfriend Gabriel Aubry. As a mother, she is particularly aware of the need for strong female role models in film and television, driving her advocacy for authentic representation of women in storytelling.

Halle Berry's advocacy extends beyond the entertainment industry; she is a vocal supporter of various causes, including domestic violence awareness, health issues, and the importance of education for young women. Berry has been open about her experiences with domestic violence, having been in a relationship that turned abusive. She has used her platform to raise awareness about the issue, emphasizing the importance of speaking out against violence and supporting victims. Berry's willingness to share her story has helped to destigmatize discussions around domestic abuse, encouraging others to seek help and support.

In addition to her advocacy for domestic violence awareness, Berry is an active supporter of health-related initiatives. She has spoken publicly about her struggles with diabetes, which she was diagnosed with in her 20s. This personal health journey has inspired her to advocate for greater awareness of the disease, particularly within the African American community, where diabetes rates are disproportionately high. Berry emphasizes the importance of education, prevention, and access to healthcare, using her own experiences to highlight the need for more resources and support for those affected by chronic health issues.

Berry's commitment to education and empowerment is also evident in her support for various organizations that focus on providing resources and opportunities for young women and girls. She believes in the power of education to transform lives and is dedicated to helping young people realize their potential. Through her philanthropic efforts, she has contributed to initiatives that provide scholarships, mentorship programs, and resources aimed at supporting the education and development of young women, particularly those from underprivileged backgrounds.

Halle Berry's advocacy is not limited to specific causes; she actively participates in broader discussions about representation and inclusivity in Hollywood. As a prominent figure in the industry, she recognizes the power of storytelling and its ability to influence societal perceptions. Berry has been vocal about the need for diverse narratives that reflect the experiences of marginalized communities, arguing that authentic representation is essential for fostering understanding and empathy. She encourages industry leaders to prioritize inclusivity in their projects, advocating for stories that showcase the rich diversity of human experiences.

Halle Berry

Throughout her career, Berry has remained committed to using her platform to advocate for change. She has consistently challenged Hollywood to expand its definition of beauty and talent, pushing back against stereotypes that have long persisted in the industry. Her advocacy for representation extends to women of all backgrounds, and she emphasizes the importance of providing opportunities for actresses of color, recognizing that diversity benefits not only the industry but also society as a whole.

Berry's personal experiences, from her childhood to her role as a mother and her advocacy for various causes, have shaped her identity as both an actress and a public figure. She embodies resilience and determination, using her voice to address pressing social issues and inspire others to do the same. Through her advocacy work, Halle Berry continues to make a significant impact, championing the rights and representation of marginalized communities in Hollywood and beyond.

Halle Berry

In summary, Halle Berry's personal life and advocacy reflect her deep commitment to social justice and representation. Her experiences as a biracial woman, a mother, and a survivor of domestic violence have shaped her perspective on the importance of authenticity and inclusivity in storytelling. Through her advocacy efforts, Berry seeks to empower others, raise awareness of critical issues, and inspire change in the entertainment industry and society at large. Her legacy as an actress is complemented by her dedication to making a positive difference in the world, showcasing the powerful intersection of personal experience and social advocacy.

CONCLUSION

Halle Berry's life story is more than an account of achievements; it is a testament to resilience, vision, and the unyielding pursuit of excellence. From her formative years in Cleveland to her status as a global icon, Berry has continuously challenged norms, shattered barriers, and inspired countless others. Her legacy is built not only on the accolades and accolades of her profession but on the countless moments where she rose against the odds and defied expectations.

The actress's journey through Hollywood has been marked by the highest of triumphs and some formidable lows. Yet, through each challenge, Berry has emerged stronger, demonstrating that true glory is not defined by a smooth path but by the strength shown in overcoming obstacles. Her story resonates because it reflects a universal truth: greatness is achieved not by avoiding hardship, but by meeting it head-on and thriving through perseverance and inner strength.

Halle Berry

As the first African-American woman to win an Oscar for Best Actress, Berry's victory in Monster's Ball was not only personal but a significant milestone for an industry still grappling with representation and diversity. But Berry's contributions extend beyond her awards. Through roles that showcased her versatility and advocacy that championed inclusion, she has carved a place for herself as an influential figure both on and off the screen.

Her journey illustrates the power of staying true to oneself and embracing one's full complexity. Berry's legacy as the "Queen of the Screen" is not merely in the roles she played but in the example she set for aspiring actors and dreamers everywhere. The portrait of Halle Berry is one of a woman who defined and redefined herself, an enduring reminder that success is the result of passion, persistence, and unwavering belief.

As we close the pages on her story, one thing remains clear: Halle Berry's impact on film and culture will

Halle Berry

continue to inspire generations. She has shown that with determination and courage, one can rise from humble beginnings to achieve unparalleled heights, becoming a beacon of hope and proof that glory is within reach for those who dare to pursue it.

www.ingramcontent.com/pod-product-compliance
Lightning Source LLC
Chambersburg PA
CBHW070115230526
45472CB00004B/1263